At Sylvan, we believe that a lifelong love of learning begins at an early age, and we are glad you have chosen our resources to help your children experience the joy of mathematics as they build critical reasoning skills. We know that the time you spend with your children reinforcing the lessons learned in school will contribute to their love of learning.

Success in math requires more than just memorizing basic facts and algorithms; it also requires children to make sense of size, shape, and numbers as they appear in the world. Children who can connect their understanding of math to the world around them will be ready for the challenges of mathematics as they advance to more complex topics.

We use a research-based, step-by-step process in teaching math at Sylvan that includes thought-provoking math problems and activities. As students increase their success as problem solvers, they become more confident. With increasing confidence, students build even more success. The design of the Sylvan workbooks will help you to help your children build the skills and confidence that will contribute to success in school.

Included with your purchase of this workbook is a coupon for a discount at a participating Sylvan center. We hope you will use this coupon to further your children's academic journeys. Let us partner with you to support the development of confident, well-prepared, independent learners.

The Sylvan Team

Kindergarten
Basic Math Success

Published in the United States by Random House, Inc., New York, and in Canada by Random House of Canada Limited, Toronto.

www.tutoring.sylvanlearning.com

Created by Smarterville Productions LLC
Producer & Editorial Direction: The Linguistic Edge
Producer: TJ Trochlil McGreevy
Writer: Amy Kraft
Cover and Interior Illustrations: Shawn Finley and Duendes del Sur
Layout and Art Direction: SunDried Penguin
Director of Product Development: Russell Ginns

First Edition

ISBN: 978-0-375-43032-9

Library of Congress Cataloging-in-Publication Data available upon request.

This book is available at special discounts for bulk purchases for sales promotions or premiums. For more information, write to Special Markets/Premium Sales, 1745 Broadway, MD 6-2, New York, New York 10019 or e-mail specialmarkets@randomhouse.com.

PRINTED IN CHINA

10 9 8 7 6 5 4 3 2

Contents

Counting to 5

Practice the Number 1

TRACE the number 1.
Start at the green arrow.

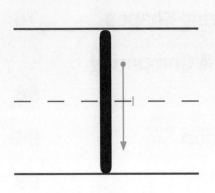
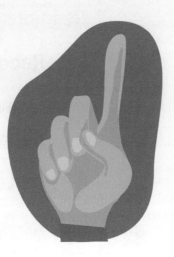

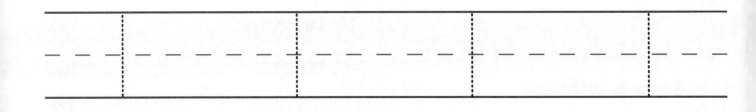

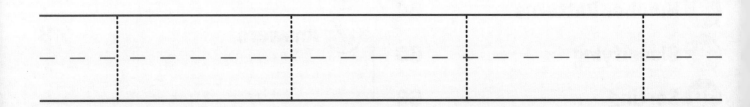

Now WRITE the number 1 next to each picture.

Practice the Number 2

TRACE the number 2.
Start at the green arrow.

Now WRITE the number **2** next to each picture.

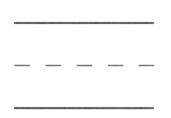

Counting to 5

Practice the Number 3

TRACE the number 3.
Start at the green arrow.

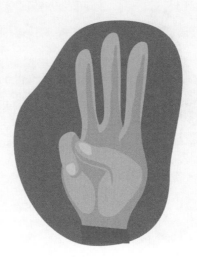

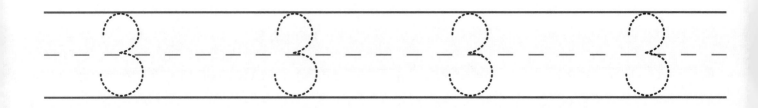

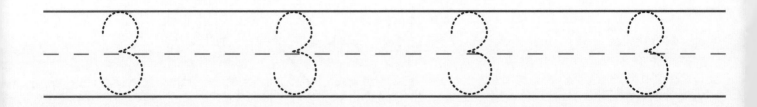

Now WRITE the number 3 next to each picture.

Practice the Number 4

TRACE the number 4.
Start at the green arrow.

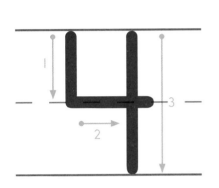

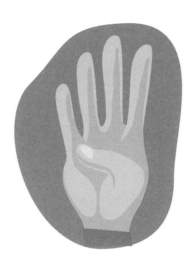

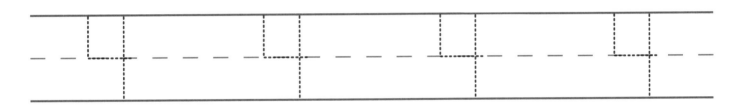

Now WRITE the number 4 next to each picture.

Counting to 5

Practice the Number 5

TRACE the number 5.
Start at the green arrow.

5   5   5   5

5   5   5   5

Now WRITE the number 5 next to each picture.

Color Groups

LOOK at each number. COLOR the correct number of pictures to match the number.

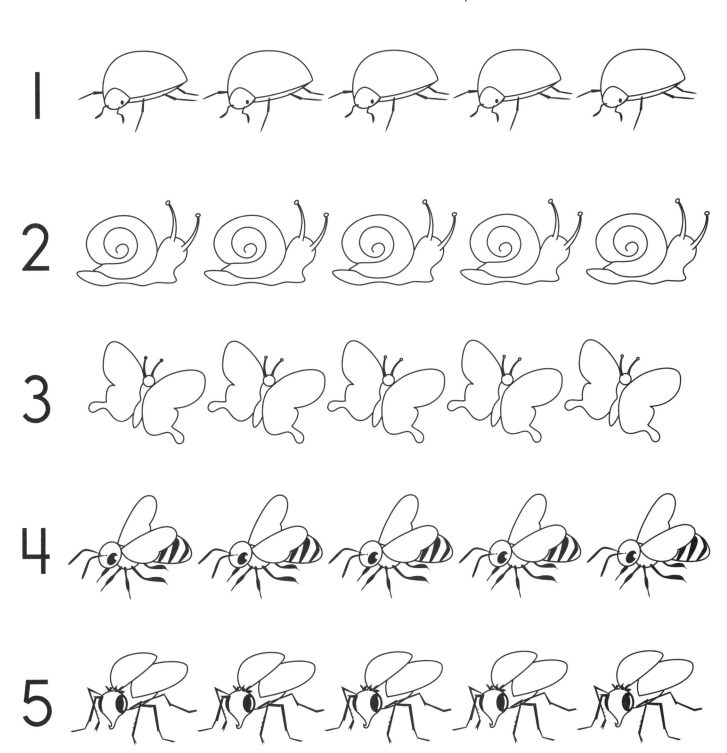

1

2

3

4

5

Magic Match Up

DRAW lines to connect the numbers and pictures that go together.

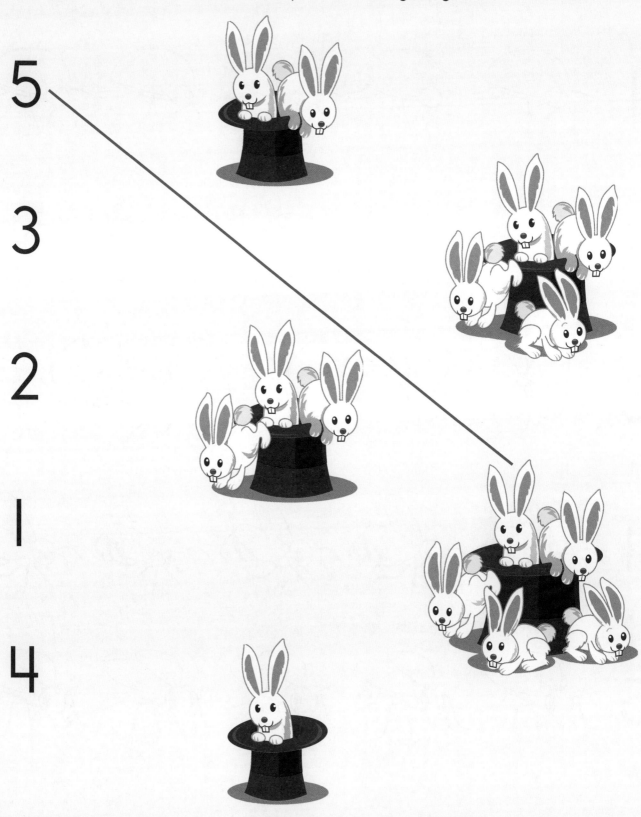

Loop It

LOOK at each number. CIRCLE the correct number of pictures to match the number.

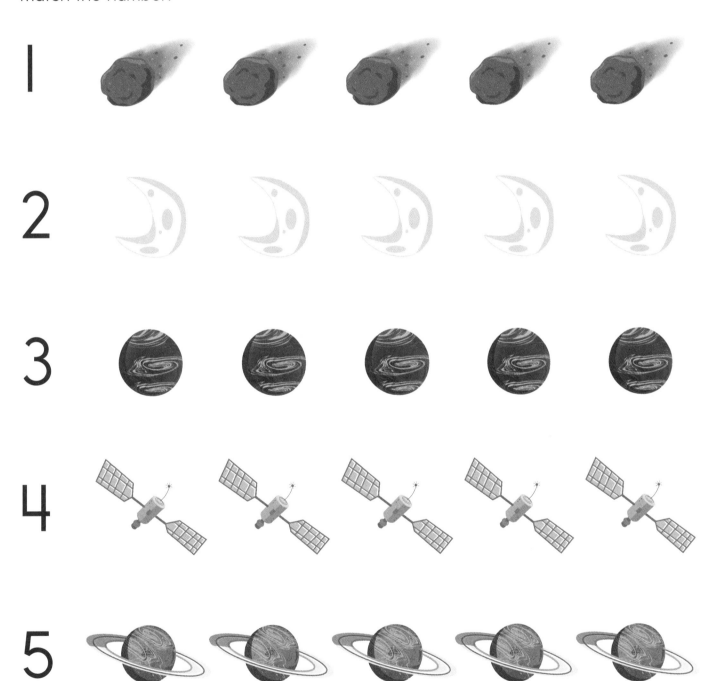

Counting to 5

Odd One Out

CROSS OUT the picture in each row that does **not** go with the others.

Hide and Seek

COUNT the number of times each object appears in the picture. Then WRITE the number next to each object.

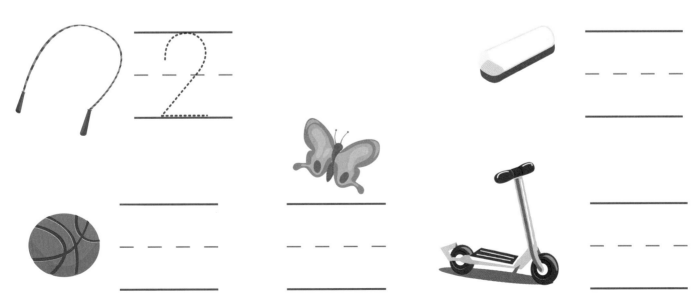

Practice the Number 6

TRACE the number 6.
Start at the green arrow.

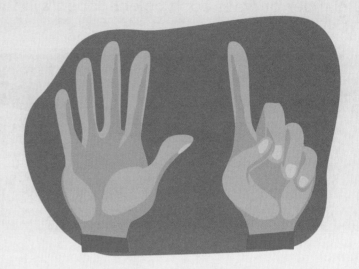

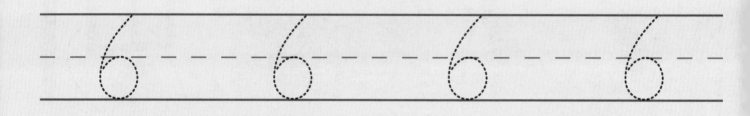

Now WRITE the number 6 next to each picture.

Practice the Number 7

TRACE the number 7.
Start at the green arrow.

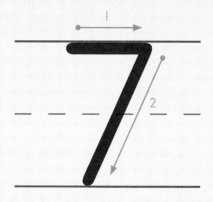

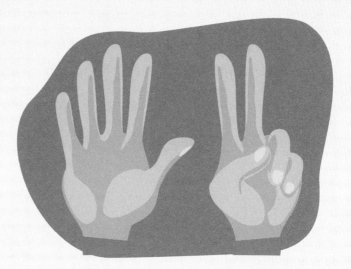

Now WRITE the number 7 next to each picture.

Counting to 10

Practice the Number 8

TRACE the number 8.
Start at the green arrow.

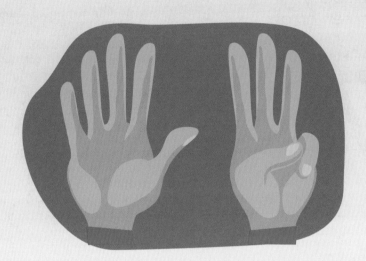

Now WRITE the number 8 next to each picture.

Practice the Number 9

TRACE the number 9.
Start at the green arrow.

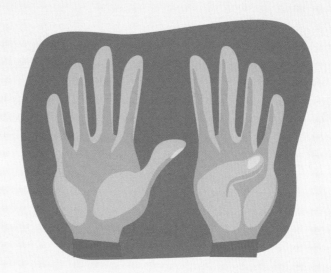

Now WRITE the number **9** next to each picture.

Practice the Number 10

TRACE the number 10.
Start at the green arrow.

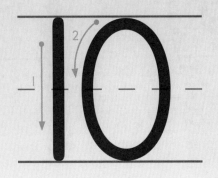

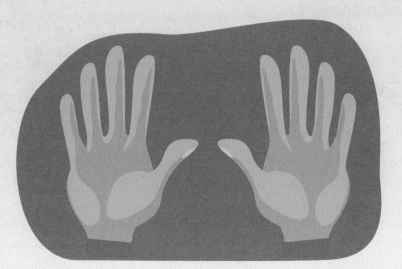

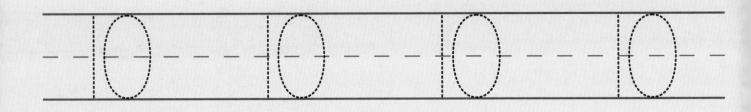

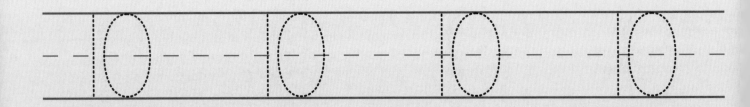

Now WRITE the number 10 next to each picture.

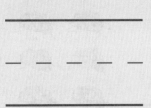

Color Groups

LOOK at each number. COLOR the correct number of pictures to match the number.

6

7

8

9

10

Fruit Match Up

DRAW lines to connect the numbers and pictures that go together.

7

8

6

10

9

Loop It

LOOK at each number. CIRCLE the correct number of jellybeans to match the number.

6

7

8

9

10

Odd One Out

CROSS OUT the picture in each row that does **not** go with the others.

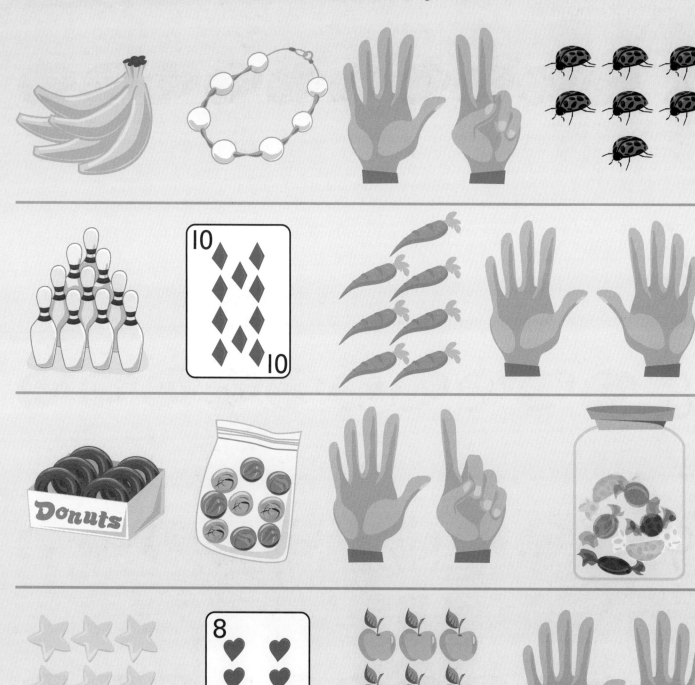

Hide and Seek

COUNT the number of times each object appears in the picture. Then WRITE the number next to each object.

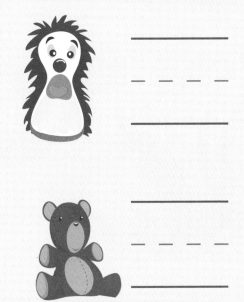

Pond Crossing

DRAW a line following the numbers 1 through 10 in order, to help the frog jump across the pond.

Card Tricks

The numbers have disappeared from the cards. WRITE the number for each card.

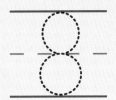

Practice the Number 0

TRACE the number 0.
Start at the green arrow.

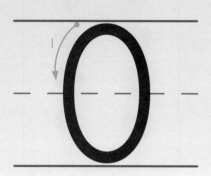

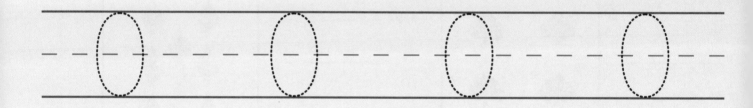

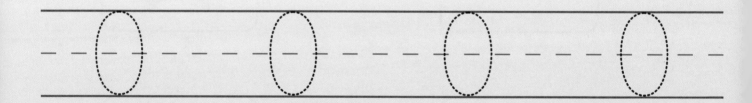

Now WRITE the number **0** next to each picture.

_____

_____

Circle the Same

CIRCLE all of the pictures that show zero.

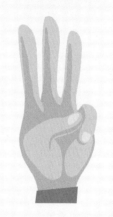

Which One Has More?

CIRCLE the group of fruit that has **more** than the other.

1.

2.

3.

4.

5.

6.

7.

8.

Hide and Seek

COUNT the number of times each fish appears in the picture, and WRITE the number next to each fish. For each pair of fish, CIRCLE the one that has **more** than the other.

Card Tricks

CIRCLE the card that has **one more** than the first card.

Which One Has Less?

LOOK at each number. CIRCLE the plate that has **one less** than the number.

4

2

6

1

Ordinal Numbers

Practice the Numbers

An **ordinal number** shows order or position, as in "*first* place." FIND each person in the picture. TRACE the ordinal number that goes with each person in line.

Color Groups

COLOR each scoop of ice cream according to the directions.

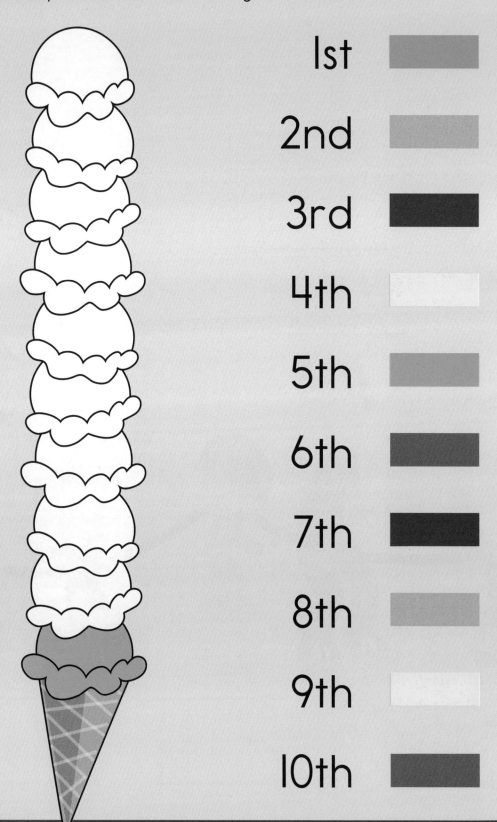

1st

2nd

3rd

4th

5th

6th

7th

8th

9th

10th

On the Shelf

CIRCLE the book cover for each position on the shelf.

1st

4th

2nd

6th

Beetlemania

LOOK at each number. CIRCLE the correct number of beetles to match that number.

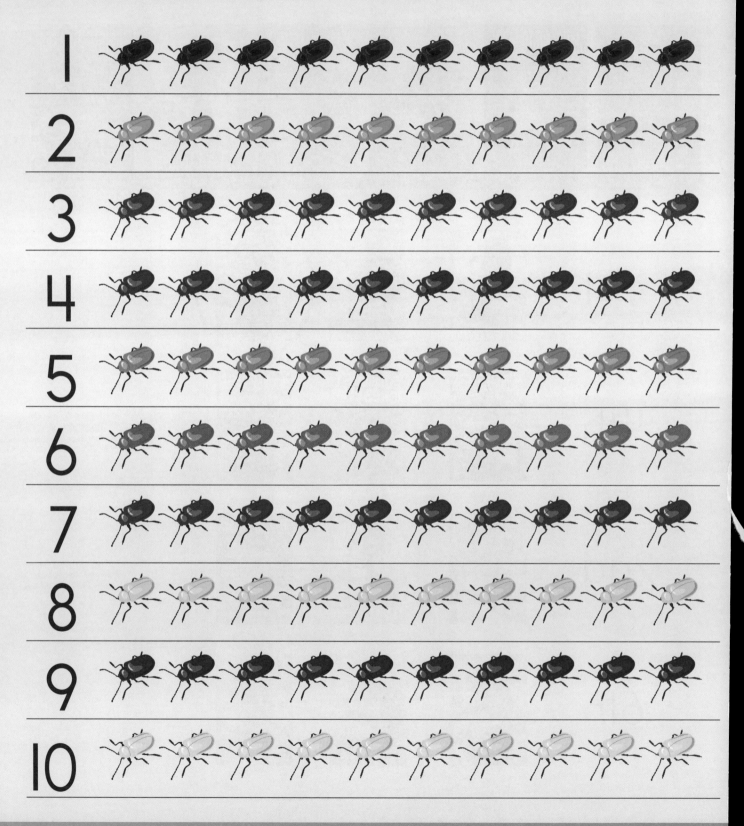

Last Place

COUNT the runners. Then WRITE the ordinal number for the place of the last runner.

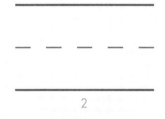

1

———————

- - - - - - -

———————

2

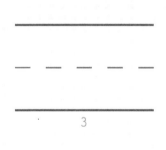

———————

- - - - - - -

———————

3

———————

- - - - - - -

———————

4

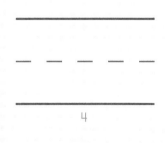

———————

- - - - - - -

———————

5

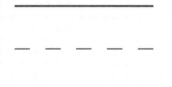

Same & Different

Circle the Same

CIRCLE the object in each row that is exactly the same as the first one.

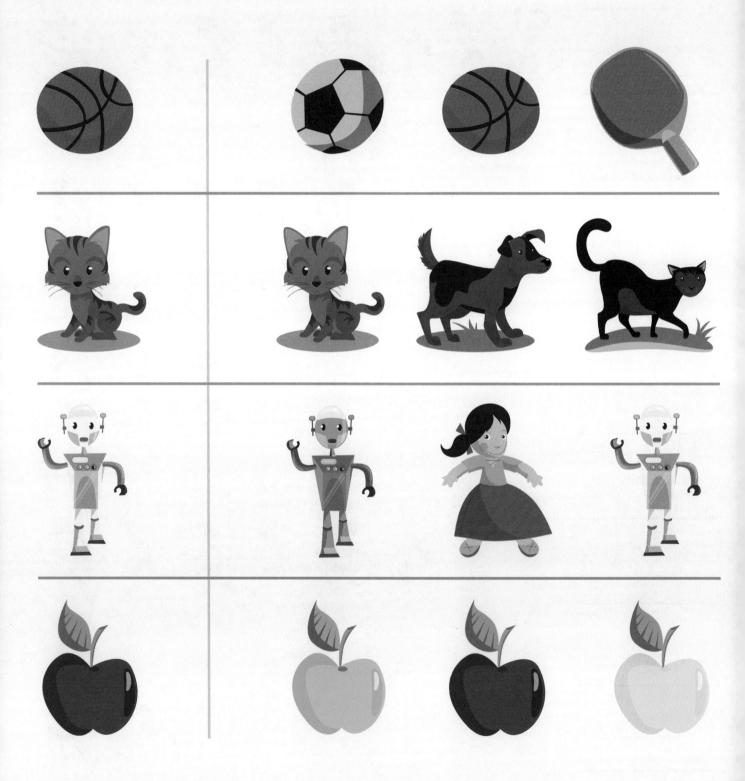

Card Tricks

CROSS OUT the pairs of cards that don't match.

Same & Different

Spot the Differences

LOOK at the two pictures. CIRCLE the differences in the second picture.

HINT: There are seven differences.

Odd One Out

CROSS OUT the picture in each row that does **not** go with the others.

Match Up

DRAW lines to connect the socks that go together.

Picture Patterns

Color the Pattern

COLOR the white boxes to finish each pattern.

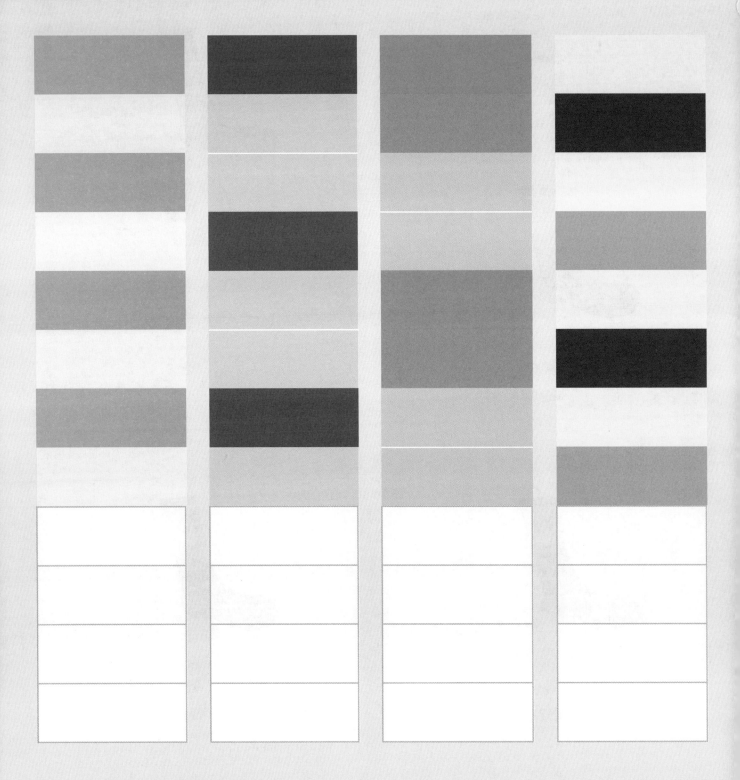

Color the Pattern

COLOR the shapes to finish each pattern.

Missing Numbers

WRITE the missing number to complete each pattern.

| 1 | 2 | 3 | 4 | 5 | 6 |

| 4 | 5 | 6 | 7 | 8 | |

| 2 | 3 | 4 | 5 | 6 | |

| | 6 | 7 | 8 | 9 | 10 |

| | 4 | 5 | 6 | 7 | 8 |

Magic Tricks

CIRCLE the picture that completes each pattern.

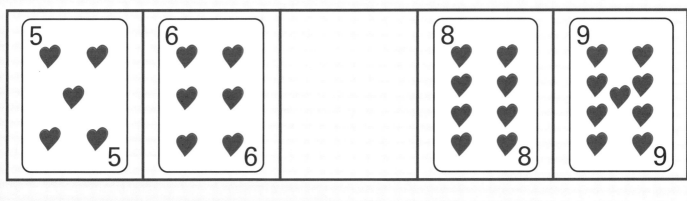

Number Patterns

What Comes Next?

CIRCLE the picture that comes next in each pattern.

1.

2.

3.

4.

Missing Buttons

WRITE the missing numbers next to the elevator buttons.

Missing Buttons

WRITE the missing numbers on the buttons.

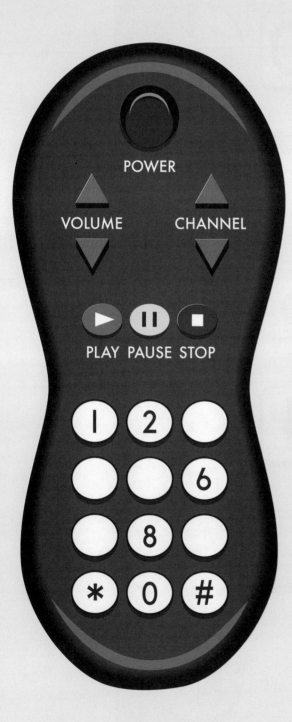

Missing Numbers

WRITE the missing numbers to complete each pattern.

Col1	Col2	Col3	Col4
1		10	
2	2	9	
	3	8	8
4			7
5	5	6	
	6		5
7		4	4
	8	3	
9	9		2
10		1	

Circle the Same

CIRCLE all of the pictures that are like the top picture.

Odd One Out

CROSS OUT the picture in each row that does **not** go with the others.

Match Up

DRAW lines to connect the numbers and pictures that go together.

8

6

3

Color Groups

COLOR each picture so that it matches the category.

Match Up

DRAW lines to connect the words and pictures that go together.

Pets

Farm
Animals

Wild
Animals

Odd One Out

CROSS OUT the picture in each row that does **not** go with the others.

Put It Away

DRAW a line to put each thing in the toy box or the toolbox.

TOOLS

TOYS

Stack Up

LOOK at the pictures. DRAW a line from each food to the shelf where it belongs.

Put It Away

DRAW a line to put each thing in the summer clothes trunk or the winter clothes trunk.

Stack Up

LOOK at the pictures. DRAW a line from each thing to the place where it belongs.

Put It Away

DRAW a line to recycle each object in the plastic or paper bin.

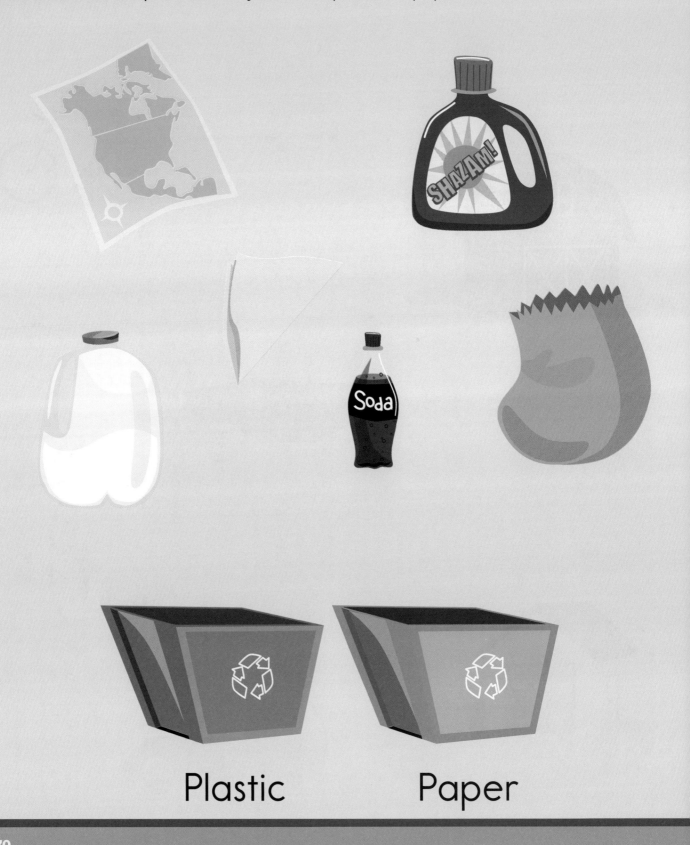

Plastic   Paper

Get in Place

DRAW a line from each picture outside the diagram to show where it belongs inside the diagram.

Beetlemania

CIRCLE the beetle that does **not** belong in each group.

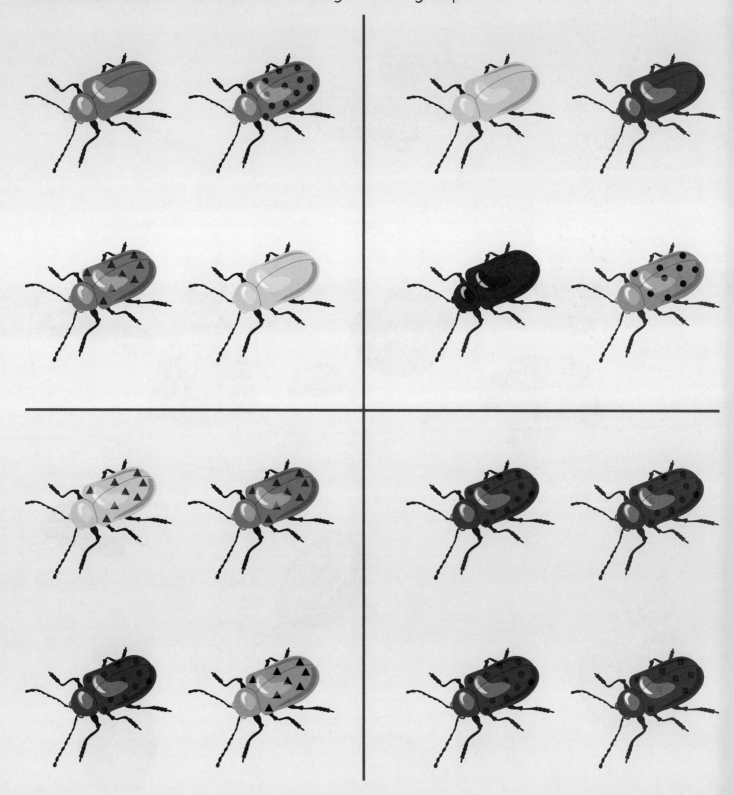

Finish the Pattern

WRITE the numbers or letters to complete each pattern.

| 1 | 2 | | 4 | 5 | | 7 | 8 |

| | 3 | 4 | | 6 | 7 | | 9 |

| 3 | | 5 | 6 | | 8 | 9 | |

| X | O | O | X | O | O | | | | | | |

| | | | X | O | O | X | X | O | O | X |

| X | X | O | | | X | X | O | X | X | O |

Beetlemania

CIRCLE the beetle that comes next in each pattern.

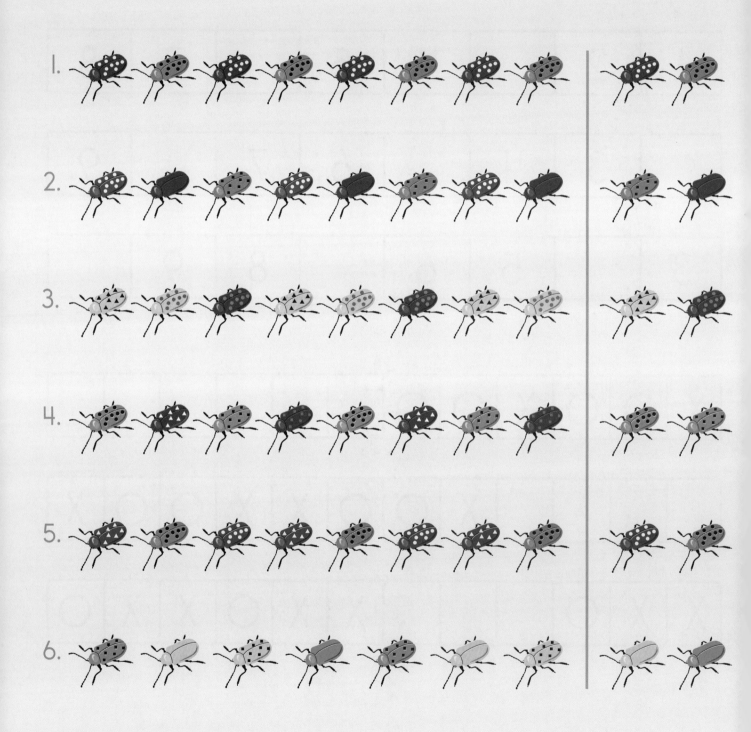

Load the Truck

DRAW a line to connect each truck with the right loading dock.

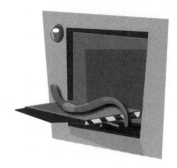

Spot the Differences

LOOK at the two pictures. CIRCLE the differences in the second picture.

HINT: There are three differences.

Color the Pattern

COLOR the shapes to finish each pattern.

Odd One Out

CIRCLE the picture in each row that does **not** go with the others.

Now WRITE what all of the circled pictures have in common.

_____

_____

_____

_____

Recognizing Shapes

Color the Circles

COLOR all of the circles.

Color the Triangles

COLOR all of the triangles.

Recognizing Shapes

Color the Rectangles

COLOR all of the rectangles.

HINT: A square is a special kind of rectangle.

Bubble Pop

LOOK at the bubbles. CROSS OUT the bubbles that are **not** circles.

Recognizing Shapes

Circle the Same

CIRCLE all of the triangles.

Pond Crossing

DRAW a line following the rectangles to help the frog jump across the pond.

HINT: A square is a special kind of rectangle.

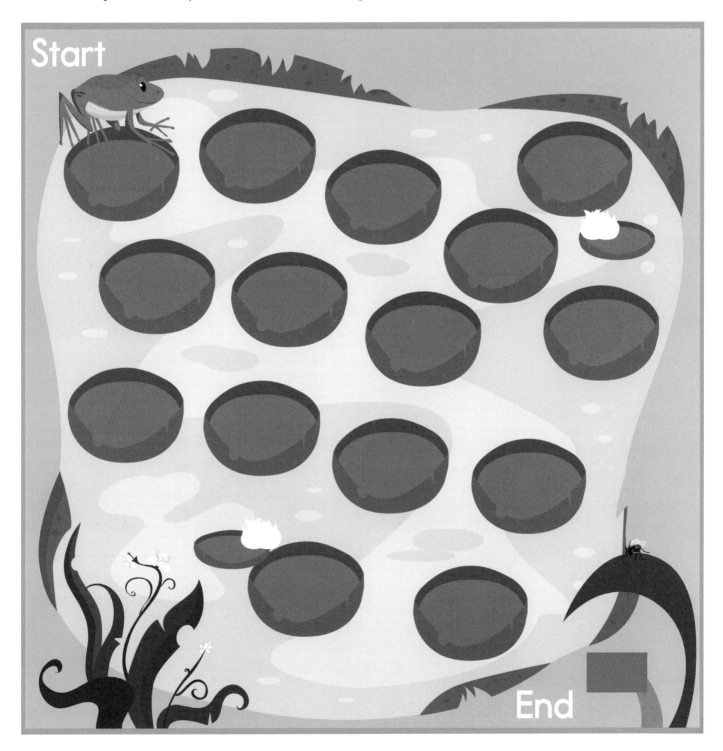

Recognizing Shapes

Circle the Same

CIRCLE the shape in each row that is the same shape as the first one.

Hide and Seek

How many of each shape can you find in the picture? WRITE the number next to each shape.

Trace and Draw

TRACE each shape. Then DRAW more of the same shape.

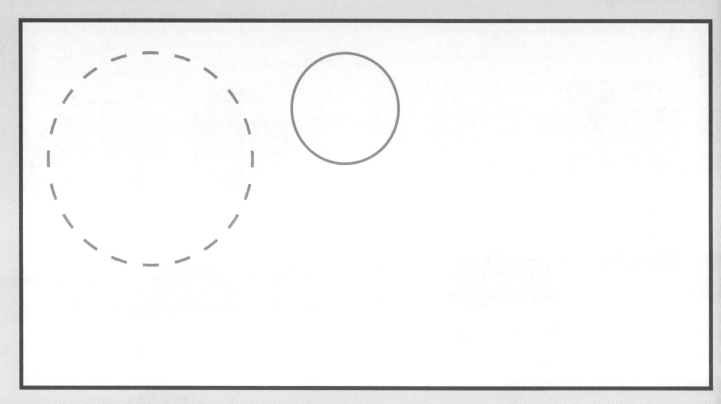

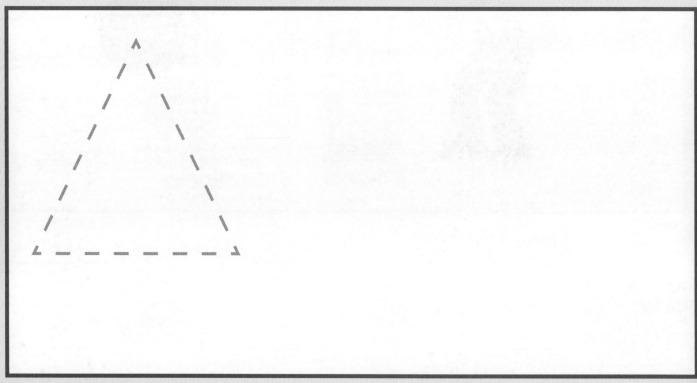

Drawing & Comparing Shapes

Small, Smaller, Smallest

CIRCLE the **smaller** shape.

CIRCLE the **smallest** shape.

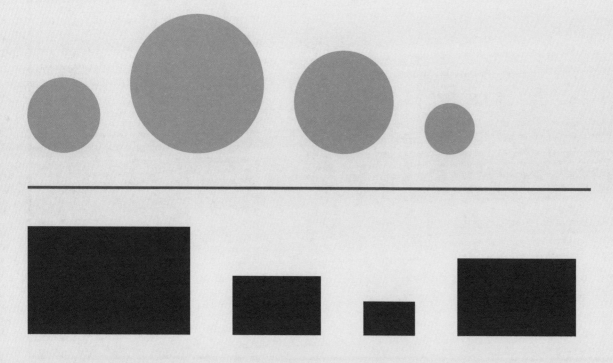

Big, Bigger, Biggest

COLOR the **bigger** shape.

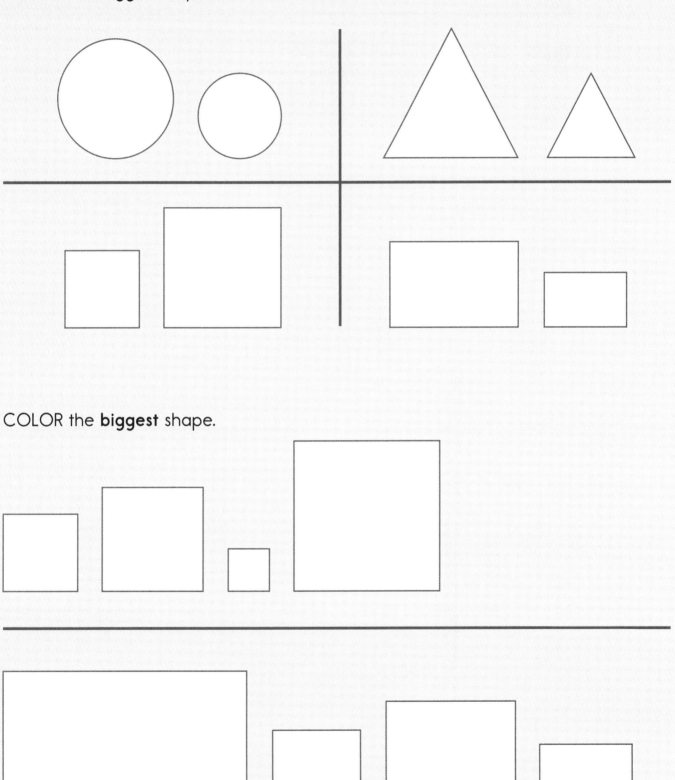

COLOR the **biggest** shape.

Drawing & Comparing Shapes

Trace and Draw

TRACE each shape. Then DRAW the same shape bigger and smaller.

Trace	Bigger	Smaller

Circle the Same

CIRCLE the shape in each row that is exactly the same as the first one.

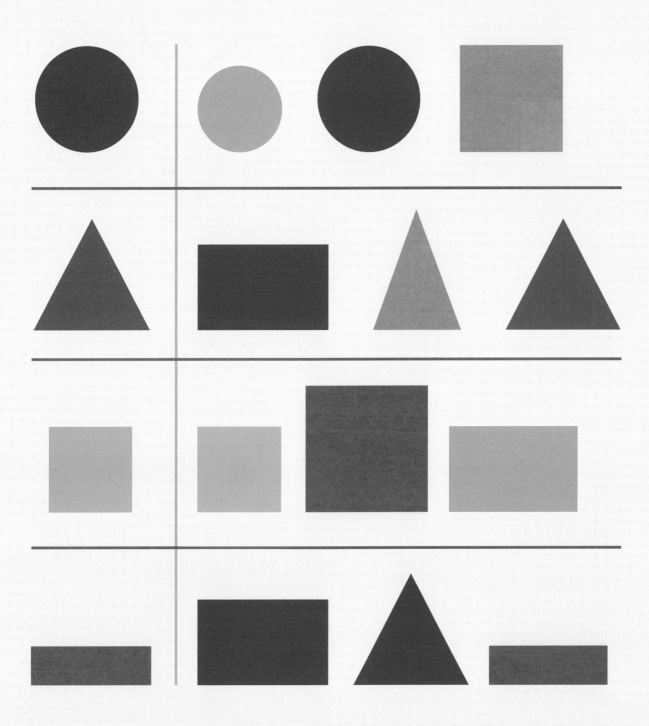

Drawing & Comparing Shapes

Match Up

DRAW lines to connect the shapes that are the same.

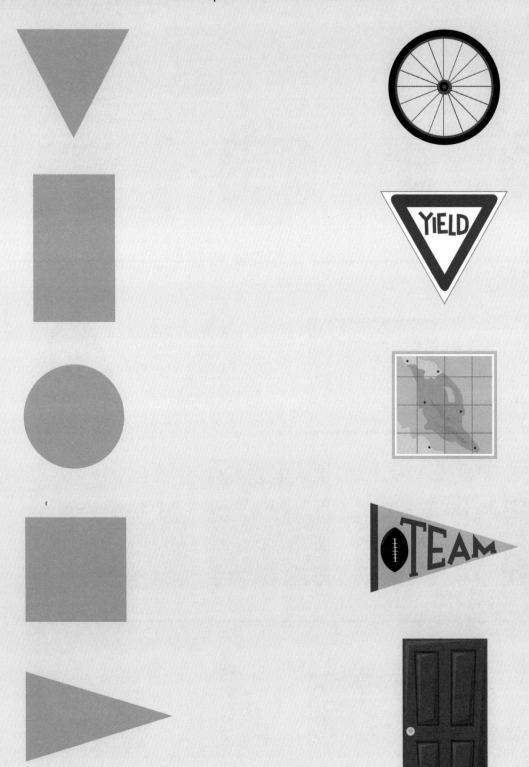

Odd One Out

CROSS OUT the picture in each row that does **not** go with the others.

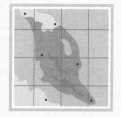   

Which One?

TRACE the triangle that is **over** another shape.

At the Market

FIND each food in the picture, and CIRCLE the food that is **under** it in the market.

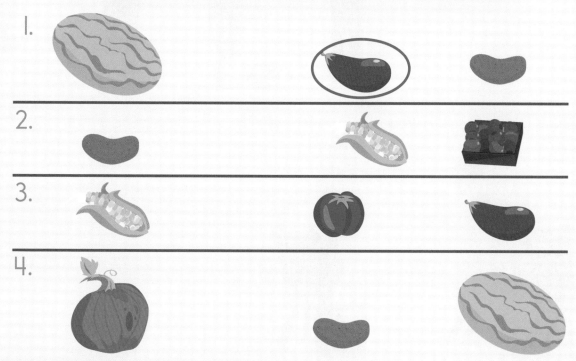

I Smell a Rat

FIND the rat in each picture, and CIRCLE the picture in each pair where the rat is **below** an object.

On the Shelf

FIND each book in the picture, and CIRCLE the book that is **above** it on the shelf.

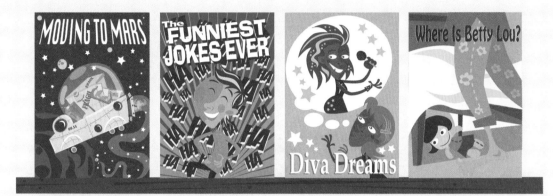

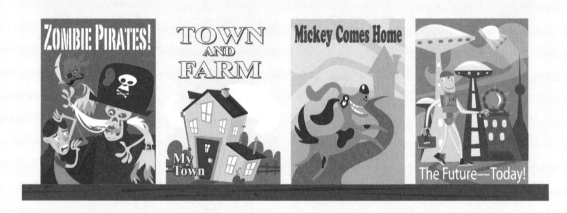

1.

2.

3.

4.

Beetlemania

DRAW a line connecting each beetle with its matching hole.

HINT: Look at the shape on each beetle's back.

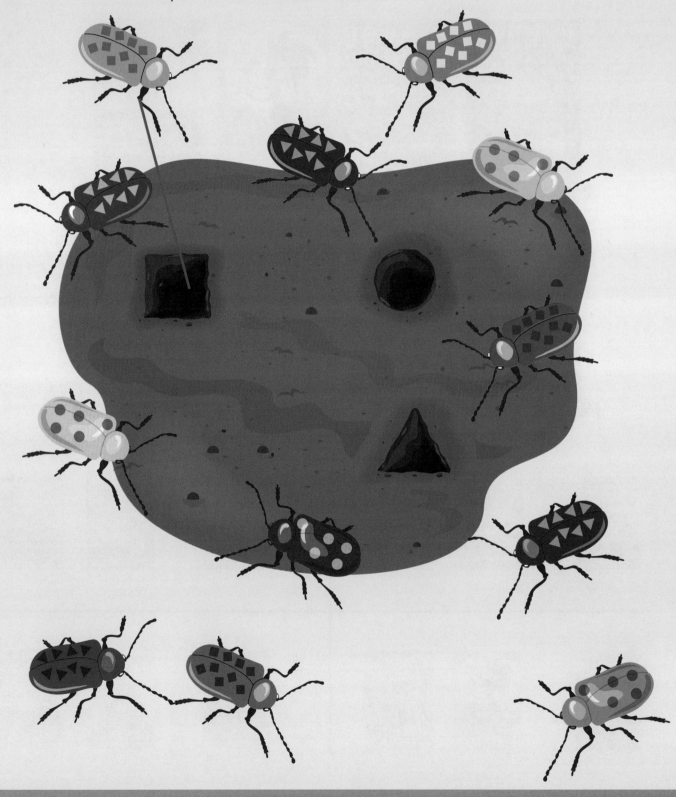

Circle It

CIRCLE the shape that matches each group of shapes.

1.

2.

3.

4.

Load the Truck

DRAW a line to connect each truck with the right loading dock.

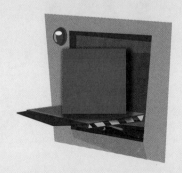

Shape Shifter

DRAW a circle below the ■.

DRAW a triangle above the ●.

DRAW a square over the ▲.

DRAW a rectangle under the ●.

Length

Which One?

CIRCLE the picture in each pair that is **longer** than the other.

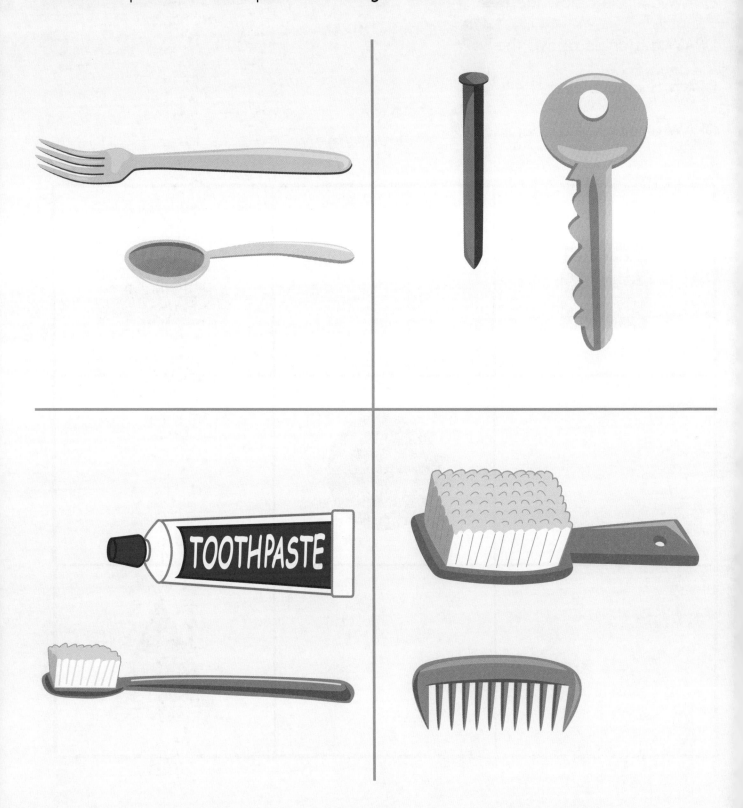

Which One?

CIRCLE the picture in each pair that is **shorter** than the other.

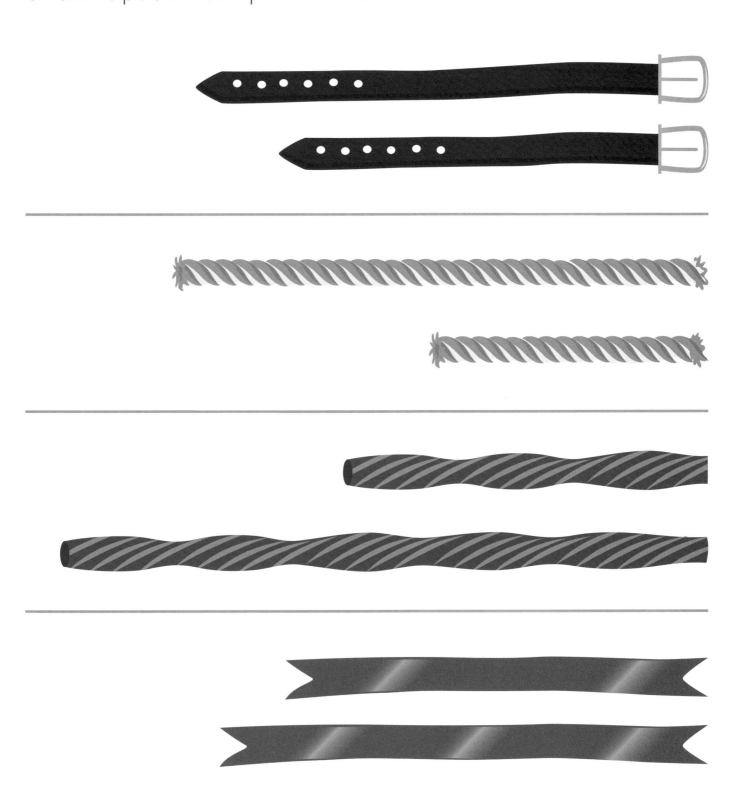

Circle the Same

CIRCLE the picture in each section that is about the same length as the top picture.

Where Will It Fit?

DRAW a line between each beam and the place where it will fit on the building.

Weight

Which One?

CIRCLE the picture of the object in each pair that is **heavier** than the other.

Which One?

CIRCLE the picture in each pair that is **lighter** than the other.

Weight

Match Up

DRAW lines to connect the objects that weigh about the same.

Can He Lift It?

The heaviest thing Jimmy can lift is a car.
CIRCLE all of the things that Jimmy can lift.

Thirst Quencher

CIRCLE the picture of the thing in each pair that holds **more** than the other.

At the Beach

CIRCLE the picture of the thing in each pair that holds **less** than the other.

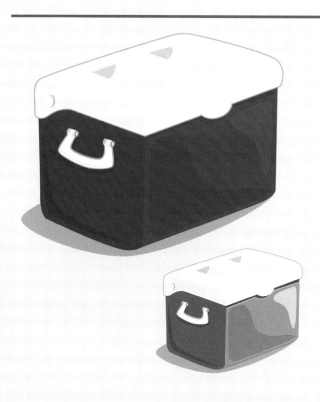

Match Up

DRAW a line between each object and the box it best fits inside.

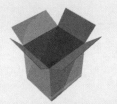

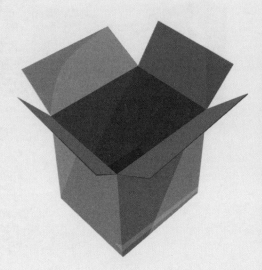

Lemonade Stand

CIRCLE the object in each pair that can hold **more** than the other.

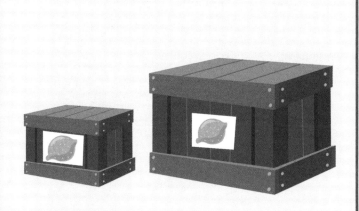  

CIRCLE the object in each pair that can hold **less** than the other.

Beetlemania

TRACE the longer line in each pair of bug trails.

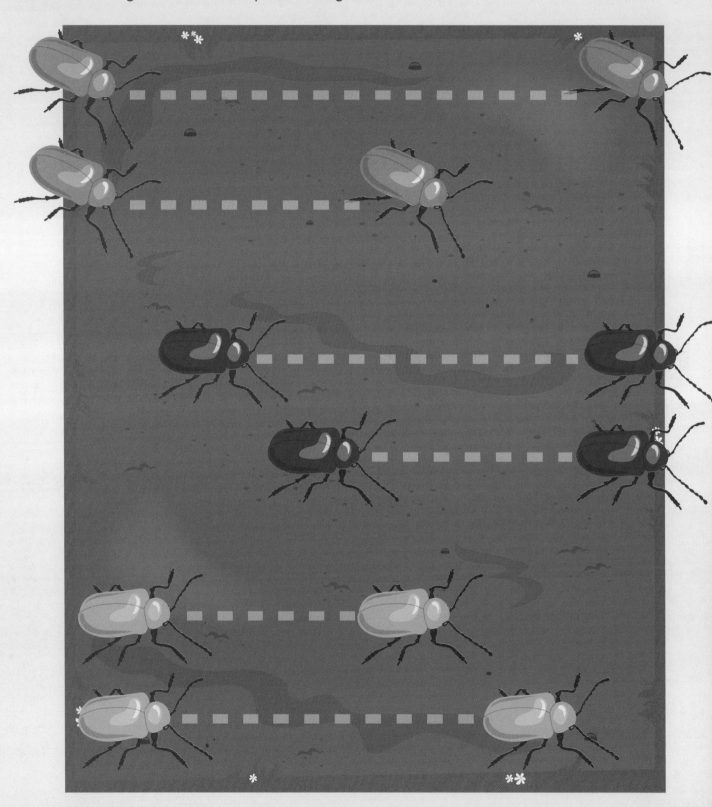

Match the Picture

DRAW a line to connect the elephant to each **heavy** object and the feather to each **light** object.

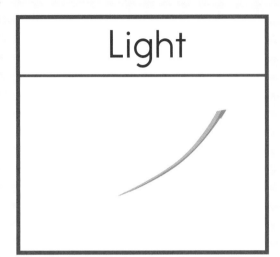

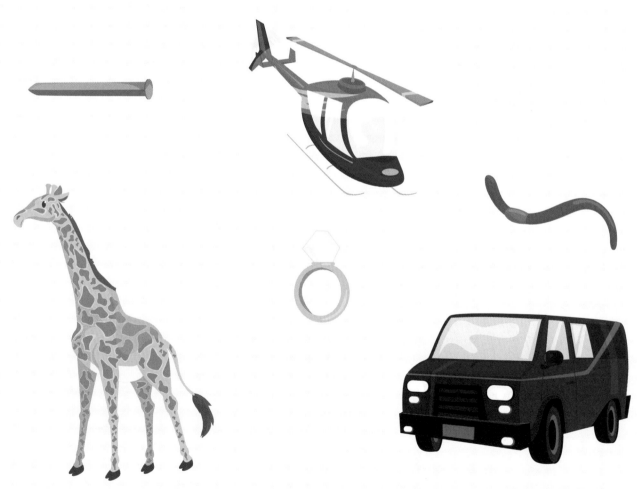

Unit Rewind

DRAW a line that is longer than the red line and shorter than the green line.

_____

_____

COLOR the object in each pair that is lighter than the other.

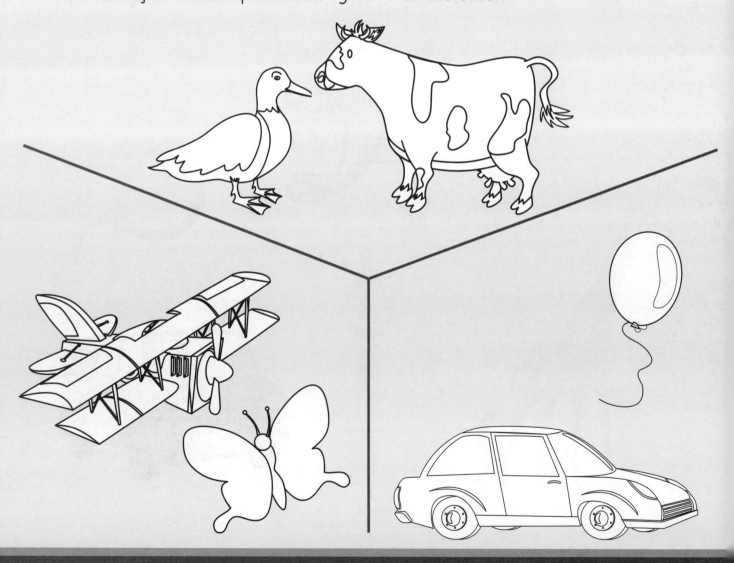

Unit Rewind

CIRCLE the object in each pair that holds more than the other.

COLOR the object in each pair that holds less than the other.

Answers

Page 7

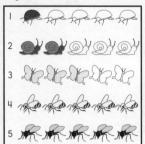
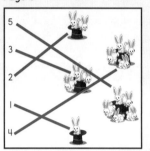
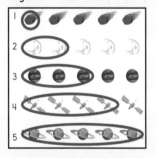
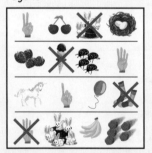

Page 8

Page 9

Page 10

Page 11

Page 17

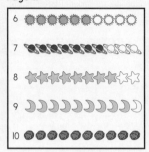

Page 18

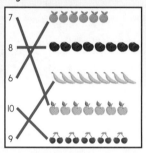

Page 19

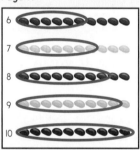

Page 20

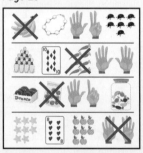

Page 21

Page 22

Page 23

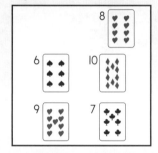

Page 25

Page 26

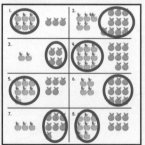

Page 27

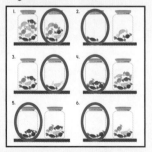

Page 28

Page 29

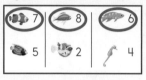

Page 30

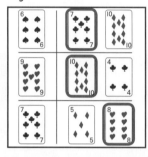

Page 31

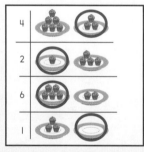

Page 34

Answers

Page 35

1st
4th
2nd
6th

Page 36

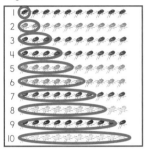

Page 37

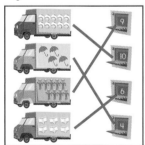

Page 38

Page 39

Page 40

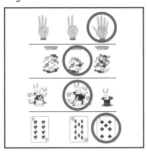

Page 41

1. 8th
2. 5th
3. 3rd
4. 6th
5. 2nd

Page 42

Page 43

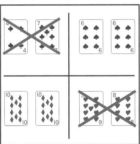

Pages 44–45

Page 46

Page 47

Page 48

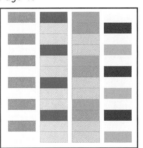

Page 49

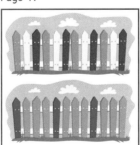

Page 50

1.
2.
3.
4.
5.

Page 51

1.
2.
3.
4.

Page 52

1.
2.
3.
4.
5.

Page 53

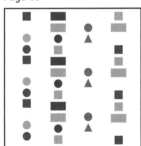

Page 54

1	2	3	4	5	6
4	5	6	7	8	9
2	3	4	5	6	7
5	6	7	8	9	10
3	4	5	6	7	8

Page 55

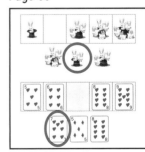

Answers

Page 56

1.
2.
3.
4.

Page 57

Page 58

Page 59

I	I	10	10
2	2	9	9
3	3	8	8
4	4	7	7
5	5	6	6
6	6	5	5
7	7	4	4
8	8	3	3
9	9	2	2
10	10	I	I

Page 60

Page 61

Page 62

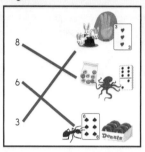

Page 63
Suggestions:

Page 64

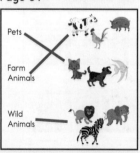

Page 65

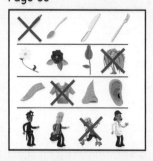

Page 66

Page 67

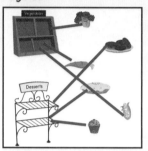

Page 68

Page 69

Page 70

Page 71

Page 72

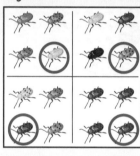

Page 73

1	2	3	4	5	6	7	8
2	3	4	5	6	7	8	9
3	4	5	6	7	8	9	10

X	O	X	O	O	X	O	O	X	O
X	O	X	O	O	X	O	X	X	O
X	O	X	O	X	X	O	X	X	O

Page 74

1.
2.
3.
4.
5.
6.

Page 75

120

Answers

Page 76

Page 77

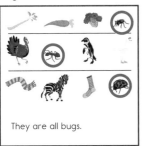

They are all bugs.

Page 78

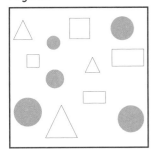

Page 79

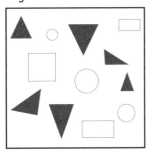

Page 80

Page 81

Page 82

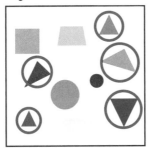

Page 83

Page 84

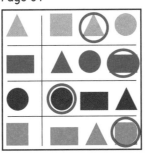

Page 85

5   3   4

Remember, a square is a special kind of rectangle.

Note: The eyes are ovals, not circles.

Page 88

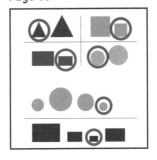

Page 89

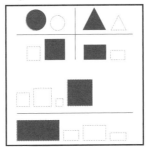

Page 90

Suggestions:

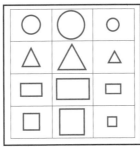

Page 91

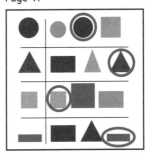

Page 92

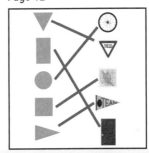

Pages 93

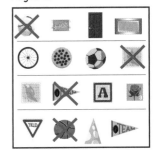

Page 94

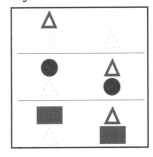

Page 95

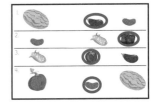

Page 96

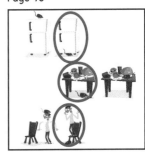

Page 97

Answers

Page 98

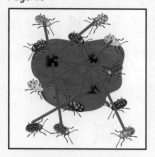

Page 103

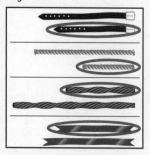

Page 108

Page 113

Page 99

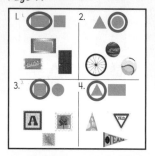

Page 104

Page 109

Page 114

Page 100

Page 105

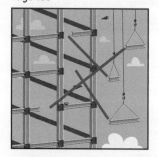

Page 110

Page 115

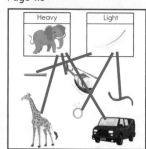

Page 101

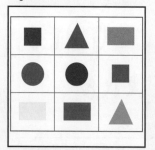

Page 106

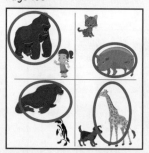

Page 111

Page 116

Page 102

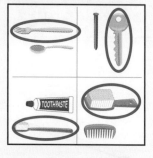

Page 107

Page 112

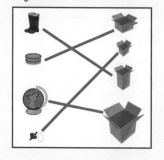

Page 117

New Sylvan Learning Math Workbooks and Super Workbooks Help Kids Catch Up, Keep Up, and

Get Ahead!

From mastering the basics to having fun with newfound skills, Sylvan Learning Math Products can help students reach their goals, whether to do better on the next report card or get ahead for the following school year.

Workbooks use a systematic, age- and grade-appropriate approach that helps children find, restore, or strengthen their math skills.

Super Workbooks include three workbooks in one low-priced package!

On Sale Now
Basic Math Success Workbooks: Grades K-5

Kindergarten Basic Math Success
978-0-375-43032-9 • $12.99/$15.99 Can

First Grade Basic Math Success
978-0-375-43034-3 • $12.99/$15.99 Can

Second Grade Basic Math Success
978-0-375-43036-7 • $12.99/$15.99 Can

Third Grade Basic Math Success
978-0-375-43039-8 • $12.99/$15.99 Can

Fourth Grade Basic Math Success
978-0-375-43042-8 • $12.99/$15.99 Can

Fifth Grade Basic Math Success
978-0-375-43045-9 • $12.99/$15.99 Can

On Sale April 2010
Math Games and Puzzles Workbooks: Grades K-5

Kindergarten Math Games and Puzzles
978-0-375-43033-6 • $12.99/$15.99 Can.

First Grade Math Games and Puzzles
978-0-375-43035-0 • $12.99/$15.99 Can

Second Grade Math Games and Puzzles
978-0-375-43037-4 • $12.99/$15.99 Can

Third Grade Math Games and Puzzles
978-0-375-43040-4 • $12.99/$15.99 Can

Fourth Grade Math Games and Puzzles
978-0-375-43043-5 • $12.99/$15.99 Can

Fifth Grade Math Games and Puzzles
978-0-375-43046-6 • $12.99/$15.99 Can

On Sale May 2010
Math In Action Workbooks: Grades 2-5

Second Grade Math in Action
978-0-375-43038-1 • $12.99/$14.99 Can

Third Grade Math in Action
978-0-375-43041-1 • $12.99/$14.99 Can

Fourth Grade Math in Action
978-0-375-43044-2 • $12.99/$14.99 Can

Fifth Grade Math in Action
978-0-375-43047-3 • $12.99/$14.99 Can

On Sale September 2010
Math Success Super Workbooks: Grades 2-5

Second Grade Math Success
978-0-375-43050-3 • $18.99/$21.99 Can

Third Grade Math Success
978-0-375-43051-0 • $18.99/$21.99 Can

Fourth Grade Math Success
978-0-307-47920-4 • $18.99/$21.99 Can

Fifth Grade Math Success
978-0-307-47921-1 • $18.99/$21.99 Can

Also available: Language Arts Workbooks, Super Workbooks, and Learning Kits for Grades K-5

 All Sylvan Learning Products include a $10 discount off a child's Skills Assessment at a Sylvan Learning Center®

Find Sylvan Learning Math and Language Arts Products at bookstores everywhere and online at:

sylvanlearningbookstore.com

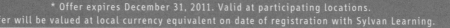